THE VALUE OF
COCONUT
MACAROONS
& OTHER STORIES

Life Lessons from a Multicultural World

THE VALUE OF COCONUT MACAROONS

& OTHER STORIES

Jay M. Poroda

with Gail "Bunny" McLeod

Cover Design by Dean Hastings

Casita
Publishing
Columbus, Ohio

The Value of Coconut Macaroons & Other Stories

Cover Design: Dean Hastings

Publisher's Cataloging-in-Publication data
Poroda, Jay M.
    The value of coconut macaroons & other stories : life lessons from a multicultural world / Jay M. Poroda with Gail "Bunny" McLeod.
    p. cm.
    ISBN 978-0-6151-9357-1
1. Poroda, Jay M. 2. Educators--United States--Biography. 3. Multiculturalism. 4. Teaching--Anecdotes. 5. Teachers--Anecdotes. I. The value of coconut macaroons and other stories. II. Title.

LA2317.P66 A3 2008
371.100924--dc22   2008901251

Printed in the United States of America

To all of my students:
Shukran, Todah, Merci, Gracias, Thanks.

To Mom and Dad:
You taught me the virtues of love, unconditional acceptance and understanding. Thank you.

CONTENTS

Introduction

"When you love people and have the desire to make a profound, positive impact upon the world, then will you have accomplished the meaning to live."

-- Sasha Azevedo

I recently attended a dinner party, and while speaking with new acquaintances, it came up in conversation that I was an educator. I know it sounds silly, but as soon as I mention this fact, I can predict the rest of the conversation.

"I remember my sixth-grade teacher, Miss May; she was a great teacher. She would always. . . ," or "My favorite teacher in high school was Mr. Jones. He really inspired me." The conversation typically progresses to how underappreciated educators are and how we have such a powerful impact on the lives of our students. It really is a scripted conversation!

That evening, the "scripted conversation" left me with a bit of an inflated ego. I began my drive home thinking, "They are right, teachers, school administrators, support staff -- we all have a huge impact on the lives of our students." As I continued my drive, my thoughts drifted to the faces of the several hundred students I have worked with during the course of my career in education, and I realized that this impact works both ways.

Throughout my career, I have had the true pleasure of meeting some of the wisest, most charming, charismatic and kind individuals. These individuals – the witch, the refugee and many others -- were my students. The lessons they presented to me in some touching, challenging and down-right silly situations have taught me to not only be a better educator, but they have also made me a better person. I can only hope that I have impacted my students as much as they have impacted and changed me.

Now when I have the "scripted conversation" regarding the impact educators have, I always add, "Yes, but what impact did you have on your teacher?"

I dedicate this book and my career in public education to all of my students. Thank you for teaching me; you have helped to make me the person I am! I love you and I appreciate you all.

"The secret of education lies in respecting the pupil."

-- Emerson

The Witch

"If you want others to be happy, practice compassion.
If you want to be happy, practice compassion."

-- The Dalai Lama

"Darby, heel," I said, trying to put some authority in my voice as I spoke, the way the student instructors in the obedience training class had said that I should. Darby wasn't having it. She was here in her home away from home and she was too busy greeting those whom she regarded as family, every bit as much as she did me. Here, by the way, was the career-technical center where I worked as a Spanish teacher and also taught English as a second language. A career-technical center offers students the required subjects for acquiring their high school diploma. Moreover, it has an emphasis on teaching work skills that will prepare students to enter into the workforce after graduation. It was here that Darby attended countless hours of obedience training.

Darby is a black Goldendoodle which is a Golden Retriever and Poodle mix. She has black curly hair and is some sixty pounds of loving wiggle. I have often remarked that Darby has more charisma than she has brains. I'm honestly not sure if this is an attribute or not.

"Darby, Darby, Darby," chanted Ricardo, a student of mine, as he got down on his knees and rubbed heads with the ecstatic dog. The two seemed to have some sort of a head butting game going which they played regularly. Since they both seemed to enjoy it and neither one seemed to get too rambunctious to the point where one or both might get hurt, I long ago decided to ignore what was happening and simply pretended not to notice.

Darby's happy-go-lucky personality and her obvious mind set of "of course everybody loves me, how can they help it?" had made her the informal mascot for the school. For many of the students in the Small Animal Care program, Darby had become a pet or at least a sort of a substitute for the pet they wished they could have. Many of them lived in situations where they couldn't have pets, with the possible exception of a goldfish or a Beta Fish and for them, Darby was a godsend.

It never failed to amaze me that no matter what language the students used when they spoke to Darby, she always seemed to understand them. Not that she would obey them any better than she would me you understand, but she didn't seem to be confused by the variety of languages with which she was addressed. Maybe it wasn't so much the words that were spoken but rather the unspoken language of the heart because it was very evident that Darby and the majority of the students had a definite love relationship going. I may call Darby my dog, and in a sense that's true, since I'm the one that gets to pay for her food, her shots and all the incidentals that go along with owning a pet, but in a much more realistic sense, Darby belongs to Darby and she shared herself indiscriminately with all of the students, faculty and staff of the career-technical center.

"Want me to take Darby down to Small Animal Care, Mr. Poroda?" asked Sharon. "I'm headed down there anyway." She tossed her head in such a way that one eye peered out from behind her barrier of long, black straight hair. Sharon looked like someone straight out of a gothic novel. Some folks have actuated Sharon with the mother in the TV program 'The Adams Family' and while this might have been true to some extent, it was not quite so. She didn't have the comedic quality of the Adams family but seemed rather more startlingly realistic, at least in keeping with realism as it is depicted in the gothic novels and movies. Since I knew that Sharon was especially fond of Darby, I had asked her recently to work with her closely in the obedience classes. I hoped that this would help Sharon to feel less insecure and not have the need to hide quite so much behind her curtain of hair and her outlandish, and in some cases intimidating, clothing and claims of witchcraft.

"Sure, Sharon, if you want to, thanks" I replied, handing her Darby's leash. The Small Animal Care facility was one of the many perks I received as a member of the faculty at the center. In order to teach the students the skills that they would need in order to successfully join the work force, the center needed customers. Since the services were being provided by students who were learning job related skills, the rates were dirt cheap which was the reason Darby was at the school with me in the first place. Darby was lovingly groomed weekly and a regular student in the obedience classes. The grooming took and Darby's black curly fur shone; it was a great testimonial for the quality of the work done in the Small Animal Care facility. As for the obedience classes, well, all I can say is that Darby is Darby, and as I remarked earlier, she has more charisma than brains.

"She really is something else, isn't she?" said James, one of my faculty colleagues, coming up beside me as I watched Sharon trying to lead Darby down the hall. Sharon was trying her best, although unsuccessfully, to get Darby to respond to the obedience lessons she had received. She would stop, firmly push Darby's rear end into sit position, then order her to heel and start off again, but

Darby wasn't cooperating. She was too busy greeting her many friends and admirers to bother with such mundane things as obedience unless she felt it was in her own best interest of course. There had been occasions when the sight of one of her favorite treats had served as an inducement to get Darby to show that she had learned a few things in her many obedience classes, at least long enough to get the treat in her possession.

I responded to what I assumed was admiration for Darby with a modest reply, "Yes, she certainly is something." Probably to convince myself that her obedience training would eventually take hold, I added some reassurance, "But she's only a year old. The books say that she's still a puppy until she reaches eighteen months so I hope she'll settle down by then and start showing that she's got some sort of brain matter between her ears."

James laughed softly. "Well, yes, her too," he admitted. "But I was speaking about our resident witch." He nodded towards Sharon. "You know she's actually got some of the students wondering about some of this witchcraft stuff she comes up with, her creepy charms and such. I wouldn't be surprised if more than one teacher wonders too if they were honest about it. Sheila told me the other day that she 'gives her the creeps'."

"I find her really interesting," I told him. "You know, there's a really sweet young girl hiding behind that hair she pulls down over her face and those black clothes and so forth. I think it's just something she hides behind, to avoid letting others intimidate her. She wants to try to intimidate them first and she covers up her insecurity with that witchcraft stuff. I'm really interested in different world religions, so I take a special interest seeing her Hollywood approach to Wicca. It's interesting to see what she'll come up with next. I'm trying to empower her a bit. I asked her to work closely with Darby in obedience training. I'm hoping it will make her feel at least a little more secure in who she is, so she won't need to hide behind some of that gothic stuff -- at least not so much."

"Well, she's got to be all right," said James. "After all, Darby likes her."

"Darby likes everyone," I objected. "That dog thinks she's the queen of the world and everyone and everything else is created for her express pleasure."

"Doesn't she just?" chuckled James as we watched Darby's many friends stopping to pet her. Although it was strictly against the rules, I knew that some of Darby's many admirers were quite apt to carry special treats on them, just in case this should be one of the frequent days when Darby came to school with me. Darby knew it too and wasn't above begging shamelessly from those whom she knew were the most likely to have one of the forbidden treats. "Doesn't she just?"

"Hey Darby, want some outrageous petting?" I asked a few days later, having finished breakfast and having a little extra time before I would need to leave for school. Darby never needs to be asked twice about outrageous petting and was immediately trying to climb into my lap. "No, Darby, down," I told her. "You're too big, way too big to be a lap dog." It was obvious that Darby didn't agree with this evaluation since she managed quite effectively to get at least a good part of herself in my lap. I began the game of outrageous petting and managed to keep at least the lower half of Darby out of my lap. "I should have given more thought to how big you would be someday when you were a baby and I let you lay up here," I told her. "But you were so darn cute."

Darby gave me a big doggy grin and tried her best to give me some of her best doggy kisses which I managed for the most part to avoid. It was evident that as far as she was concerned she still was 'so darn cute' and although I hated to admit it, I thought so too. I continued petting Darby and in doing so I suddenly became aware of a large mass growing on one of her hind legs. "Hey, what've we got here, girl?" I asked her, carefully feeling of the lump. My touching it didn't seem to be causing Darby any pain, but I decided it would probably be a good idea to schedule an appointment to take her to the vet, just to have him take a look. "About time you went in for a checkup anyway, girl," I told her.

I called the vet and told him what I had found and was rather surprised when he suggested that I bring her right in that morning on my way to work. "That way, if it looks like anything we need to be concerned about, you can leave her here and we'll take some tests," he told me. "It's smart to get right on top of these things, just in case."

Maybe it was some sort of denial shield that I put up in my mind, but I really didn't expect the lump to be anything important. I really expected that the vet would look at it, declare it to be of little or no importance and that Darby and I would continue on our way to the center, as we did every other day when Darby went to work with me. "It's a cyst," the vet told me. "It may be cancerous, then again it may not be. The only way to make an accurate diagnosis is through some further tests, so why don't you leave her here with me and then pick her up on your way home?"

Needless to say I was a mess. "Not Darby, please, not Darby!" I said goodbye to Darby, doing my best not to let my voice break so that she'd suspect anything was wrong.

I got to the center, parking in my usual spot, and went into the building. Since this was Wednesday, a day when Darby regularly came with me, her absence was conspicuously noticeable. I felt as if I was in some sort of a trance, a twilight zone if you will, going through the usual motions of living but someplace else at the same time. I couldn't get my mind off of Darby; Darby as a baby, with her chubby little puppy legs, Darby tipping over her dish of milk, Darby as she had been at different stages through the past year. Darby, Darby, Darby. I saw several people start to approach me and then stop and head in another direction. I was fighting back the tears and I'm sure the anguish must have shown on my face. I saw the question in their glances, but no one came up and asked. Perhaps they were afraid of what they would find out.

I took my place in the front of the classroom as I tried to teach my first period Spanish III class. I knew that the students realized something was wrong, seriously wrong, because I was choking back my tears all through that first period.

Sharon waited until the rest of the class had left the room and then approached my desk. "Where's Darby?" she asked.

I strove to gain control of myself. I felt the tear that ran down my cheek as I responded and brushed it away quickly; after all, we're taught, almost from babyhood that men don't cry. Personally, I don't regard tears as a sign of weakness, but many do and I wanted to appear as a strong role model for my students. Sharon was one of my students and I had to put her needs ahead of my own. On the other hand, I knew that Sharon loved Darby as much, or at least nearly as much as I did, and I felt she had a right to ask the question and to know the truth.

"Darby's at the animal hospital," I told her, my voice breaking as I struggled against the sobs.

"They're doing tests. The vet said it may be cancer." I broke down and told Sharon the whole story, how I had found the lump that morning and how the vet had me bring Darby right in. "So if it is cancer, I'm going to have to make some difficult decisions," I finished, trying to pull myself together and sound like a positive adult. I felt again the eerie experience as if I were in some sort of a twilight zone. "Dear God," I thought. "This can't be happening, not to Darby, not to me." I took a deep breath and then continued. "I don't want Darby to suffer, but on the other hand I don't want to, I can't. . . ." I broke off, unable to continue.

I heard the quick intake of breath as I mentioned cancer, then silence. Sharon put her hand on my shoulder and said in a completely positive tone of voice, "It will be ok." Then she left for her next class.

The next morning Sharon entered my classroom right after I unlocked the classroom door. It was evident she had been watching for me. "This is for Darby's good health," she told me, handing me an object. I looked down. It was a VOODOO doll! Sharon had taken a black stuffed dog, a Beanie Baby® sort of thing and bound it with red silk cording, interspersed with Chinese coins and a few Spanish coins, most likely because I was her Spanish teacher. "Sharon didn't make this gift to intimidate me," I thought to myself, but to show compassion and to comfort me, much as someone else might say, "I'll be praying for Darby." This was Sharon's prayer.

9

"Thank you," I said simply. The words didn't seem enough, but there were no others that could adequately express what I was feeling.

Darby's cyst turned out to be only a fatty mass, something easily taken care of, but Sharon's Voodoo doll still sits on my desk, not as a good luck charm, but as a constant reminder that while we may not always understand a student's beliefs or behaviors, we must always search for and celebrate the worth and dignity of each student.

May it ever be.

Teachers, Turn in Your Grade Books

"Human diversity makes tolerance more than a virtue;
it makes it a requirement for survival."

-- Rene Dubos

"This is fantastic," I said to my colleagues. "I can't believe how smoothly everything is going." 'This' was *The American Mosaic*, an interdisciplinary unit that we, the members of the Foreign Language department had put together. It was designed to give our students insight into the many cultures that make up the American landscape by having them participate in a variety of fun, hands-on cultural activities.

11

"I can't believe those African dancers," said Philomena, "dancing in and out of those branches while the kids were beating out the rhythm with them. I would have been so scared they'd get mixed up on the beat and I'd get a broken ankle."

"As long as the kids remember four vertical hits, then two horizontal hits they're fine," said Norma.

"Yes," laughed Philomena, "as long as they remember. That's the problem. I'd be afraid they'd forget or get mixed up. And barefooted too." She pretended to shiver. "That wouldn't be for me, thank you very much."

"Hopefully this will help the kids to see the value and wonder of living in a multicultural world," said Norma. "If only they can see that we don't have just one culture in our country! Instead we have a number of cultures who live together."

"Maybe with special events like this, we can help them to truly appreciate and embrace the diversities that we have, to value the differences that make up this country," I replied.

It was a warm, sunny morning in May 2000. Not only was the sun shining, but it was also my department's day to shine. The day had been amazing. Students had played multicultural games, eaten ethnic foods, listened to guest speakers, watched and taken part in traditional African dancing. More than 700 students had participated in the activities we had developed. The day had gone fantastically well. The students were all back in their homerooms and we were wrapping up our activities for the day.

"Teachers, please turn your grade books into the office," came the voice of Silvia, our Assistant Principal. There was urgency in Silvia's voice that I had never heard before, and it made the announcement seem ominous.

My heart fell into my stomach. "Good God, this can't be happening," I thought to myself. "Please, let this be just some sort of a drill to make sure that everyone is right on the ball as to what we're supposed to do if something like this happens." I hurried over to the doors, trying to give the appearance of not hurrying and locked them, and then I strolled over to the windows and pulled down and closed the blinds, talking to my students all the time as I did so, trying to convey an atmosphere of normalcy. You see, those words were the signal for lockdown. This meant that we were to lock all interior and exterior doors, to evacuate the hallways and to account for each student. If this wasn't some sort of a drill, as I prayed it was, then something was wrong, seriously wrong, and our lives, the life of every student and staff member might well be in danger. I quickly took an attendance count, thankful to see that each student was present.

"I've got to stay calm," I told myself. "I don't want to tell the students that there is an emergency situation until it is absolutely necessary. They're going to panic when they realize." I was wrong. When the time for dismissal came, the bell didn't ring and there were no sounds from the corridors of other classes being dismissed, I could see the looks of fear, horror and apprehension coming over the faces of my students, but they all sat quietly. I saw one girl quickly wipe away a tear and then fold her hands back down on the desk in a posture of undivided attention, as if nothing unusual was happening.

"Mr. Poroda, what's going on?" asked one boy finally. All eyes were upon me, waiting for my answer. The silence was thunderous.

I tried to make my voice sound calm and reassuring," I don't know, but I do want you to know that we are all completely, 100% safe where we are; don't worry," I answered.

"Thanks," he answered. He smiled gently, not out of relief, but with an unspoken recognition of my concern.

"So, can anyone tell me what they especially liked about today's activities?" I asked, sitting down on the edge of my desk and trying to keep everyone's mind occupied with something other than what might or might not be going on.

The students responded in kind, talking about things they had especially liked about the day and what they would like to have seen done differently. Their voices may have been stilted, their talk contrived, spoken to help their classmates feel less frightened, but they all arose to the occasion, valiantly being there for each other. They earned my respect and admiration as they did so. Somehow I would not have expected them to conduct themselves in this manner, with this sort of bravery and maturity. This situation continued for about ten minutes after the regular dismissal time. The bell rang and the students left the building without incident. Ten minutes that felt like a hundred hours.

I stood by the doorway to my classroom and watched as students left the building, a normal everyday occurrence even though it occurred some ten minutes later than usual. "Thank God, thank God," I thought to myself. The realization of what this could have been began to sink in and the sense of horror and fear with which I was touched earlier was nothing in comparison with what I was now feeling. I searched frantically to discover what had really happened. Underneath the normalcy, one could sense a feeling of something else, something colored by a feeling of what might have been, of wonderment as to what had happened and a feeling of desperate determination to find out what had transpired during the time we were in a state of lockdown.

Tom, one of my faculty colleagues, came over to stand beside me. "Did you hear what happened?" he asked me.

"No, nothing. Do you have any idea?"

"Yeah," he answered. He remained silent for a moment. "You know Baumhammers, Richard Baumhammers, the immigration attorney who lives near the school?"

"Yes, I know who you mean," I told him. I waited to hear what he was going to say. Wanting to know, yet dreading what I was about to find out, I listened in frozen silence.

"He went on a shooting spree," said Tom. Killed five people and hurt another one pretty badly." He stood silently for a moment.

14

"Racial thing," he added. He sighed deeply, staring off into space. He continued, "He killed two men at an Indian grocery, drove to a gym and shot an African-American man, and then went and killed two Asian men at a Chinese restaurant. They said he also shot and damaged several synagogues. My God, Jay," he stopped and just shook his head. "I can't believe it; I know it's true, but I just don't want to believe it. I want to just go out the door and have it be normal like every other day yet I know it's not going to be."

Luckily none of my students or none of the schools were directly affected by this tragedy. Ironically, the incident seemed to tie in with our diversity activities, showing in a stark way what hatred and prejudice, any kind of hatred and prejudice, could mean in contrast to what we had spent the day learning.

Lady Liberty's Robe

"True friendship is felt, not said."

-- Mariecris Madayag

"Hey, that doesn't quite meet the school dress code, does it fellas?" I asked as Justin and Matt, two seventh grade students, when they passed me in the hall. They both were wearing oversized shirts, semi buttoned in the back over their regular school clothes. I knew full well the reason behind the unusual attire, but I just wanted to stop and joke with the two boys for a moment.

"These are our artists' smocks, Mr. Poroda," said Justin, holding his arms out straight from his sides and turning around in a circle so that I could get the full effect. Matt grinned as he watched his friend model the shirt for me. Matt was somewhat shy, especially when it came to talking to adults, but it was evident that he was clearly enjoying his friend's parody.

Justin and Matt were the best of friends. What made this friendship unusual was the fact that they were complete opposites! Justin was outgoing, creative, musical and had a tremendous interest in the arts. Matt, on the other hand, was somewhat shy, athletic and fanatical about sports, namely baseball and soccer.

"We decided to join the same after school clubs so that we could hang out together," explained Justin. "We each chose one. I chose art and Matt chose baseball and so we signed up for both of them. It will broaden our horizons," he told me, a spark of mischief in his eyes as he tried not to grin. I had to bite my own lip to keep from laughing. I knew exactly what teacher he was mimicking and I felt it probably wouldn't be appropriate if I laughed. Justin and Matt had a very special friendship. Because of their mutual respect and liking for each other, they were able to learn from each other and to grow as individuals.

"We've been assigned to work on the mural, Mr. Poroda," said Matt. "We're doing the Statue of Liberty part; it's a big old thing."

"It is eight feet high," added Justin. "We have to climb up on stepladders to do part of it. It's supposed to show diversity in the United States. The mural is going to be really cool."

"Mrs. Barnhart said it would show what makes the United States strong as a nation, our diversity," said Matt. "Hey, speaking of Mrs. Barnhart, we'd better get going or we're going to be late."

"I'll be seeing you down by the mural in a little while," I told them. "I promised Mrs. Barnhart I'd be around to see if there was anything I could do to help."

I already knew the facts on the mural, quite a bit about it actually, since Amy Barnhart, an art teacher at the school, and I had come up with the original idea for it in the first place. Our original idea had mushroomed into this tremendous project and I couldn't have been happier although I will admit that there were times when I felt like a father whose child had suddenly started crawling away from him faster than he could keep up.

The school had contacted Joe Servelo, who was an award winning artist and illustrator. He had agreed to serve as the technical consultant for this project. He had done other such work previously with great results so I was really excited about his involvement with our project. He had come to the school to help the students design the mural and to show them the technical processes of mural painting. As Matt had said, the mural became an 8' x 32' commemoration to show what makes us strong as a nation, our diversity. Before the mural was completed, we expected to involve literally hundreds of students.

When I joined the painting club a little later, I saw that Matt and Justin were busily working away. Justin was creating the basic framework to depict the Statue of Liberty, and Matt was helping him fill in the details.

Two weeks into the project, while the mural was still at a very basic stage, I noticed Justin working alone on the section which had been given to him and Matt. "Where's Matt?" I asked.

"Oh, he is home sick today with a sore throat, he should be here tomorrow Mr. Poroda," answered Justin.

"That's too bad," I told him. "Please tell him I said hi and that I hope he's feeling better."

"Sure, Mr. Poroda," said Justin. "I'll be sure and do that. I'm going to call him when I get home. If he's feeling ok, we'll probably play some online games on our computers. After we get our homework done of course," he added hastily.

"Of course," I told him and continued on my way, monitoring the students on completion of their assigned components of the mural.

Shortly after I arrived at work at 7:00, I began to prepare my lessons for the day. An announcement came over the PA system; it was our building principal. "Staff, please report to the auditorium at this time for a brief, but extremely important faculty meeting.

I quickly arrived at the faculty meeting and noticed that Mr. Davis, our school principal, was visibly upset. We waited a few minutes until all staff arrived, and the principal finally spoke. "Staff, I received a phone call this morning from Mrs. Smith, Matt's mother," he told us. He hesitated. It was evident that he was finding it hard to go on. "On Monday Matt was diagnosed with strep-throat. Unfortunately, the strep traveled into Matt's kidneys and he passed away last night." His voice broke as he finished speaking.

"How can this be happening?" I thought. "Matt, he's a healthy 12 year old boy. These things don't happen to kids." Yet all the time I knew that what I had just heard was true and that yes, unfortunately these things do happen to kids.

The rest of the meeting involved informing us of the appropriate procedures to follow in a situation like this, such as telling us what we could and could not say to the students, telling us about counseling services that would be available for the staff and students, as well as telling us about funeral arrangements that were being made by the family.

Needless to say, Justin was devastated; he had literally lost his best friend. We continued working on the mural in order to provide the kids with a sense of normalcy and routine, and Justin worked even more diligently on Lady Liberty. We refrained from assigning someone to help Justin on that section. He didn't ask for any help and somehow we felt it would be better to let things remain as they were. We noticed that some of the kids would leave their parts of the mural occasionally and go over to talk with him and to help him a little bit. They sensitively supported Justin so that he would be on target for his part of the mural. Kids can be pretty great and rise to the occasion when a situation requires it, and it seemed best to let them handle this in their own way.

Two months passed, and we finally unveiled the mural in front of an audience of the students' friends and families, staff members and local business leaders who donated the supplies for the mural's completion.

After the unveiling, Justin pulled Matt's mother and me aside. "Mrs. Smith, Mr. Poroda, I made the Statue of Liberty as tribute to Matt," he told us.

"Yes, Justin, I know," I told him. "You worked really hard on your piece of the mural; Matt would be proud."

"No. The Statue of Liberty really is a tribute to Matt. Look!" As I looked carefully at the painting, I noticed that the folds of Lady Liberty's robe spelled Matt's name. It was done in a very inconspicuous manner, the kind of thing one wouldn't be apt to notice unless one knew it was there, but once seen you couldn't miss it. At the very base of the statue was painted a small baseball.

Mrs. Smith hugged Justin and simply said, "Thank you." There really weren't any other words that could have expressed her feelings, those two said it all.

Eating Alone

"The free expression of the hopes and aspirations of a people is the greatest and only safety in a sane society."

-- Emma Goldman

When I was an assistant high school principal, I had the pleasure of working with Lori, a student everyone admired. She was the sort of person that just seemed to be at ease with people and to genuinely care about everyone she came in contact with. She always seemed to be in the midst of a group, always at the center of whatever activity she was taking part. She was active in sports as well as in other activities. To one looking on, she would seem to have had the ideal student life.

During her junior year, Lori made a major life decision. She decided to come out of the closet. She didn't make it a big deal; she decided to just no longer hide the fact that she was a Lesbian.

Suddenly things changed. From being the center of a crowd, Lori found herself being shunned. From being at a crowded table in the cafeteria, Lori suddenly discovered that she was being ostracized, and began to eat alone. It was terrible. I hurt for her, but I was at a loss to know what to do. There was no way I could use my authority to make kids like her. Oh, a few well-placed words could probably have resulted in some students joining her at the table, but she would still have been eating alone. Eating alone at a crowded table would have been far worse than eating alone at a table of one.

I observed the situation without seeming to. I saw Lori eating alone in the cafeteria, day after day, while the folks, whom she formerly called friends, avoided having any contact with her. I gave a lot of thought as to whether or not I should acknowledge what was happening to her. Finally I went to her and said, "Lori, if it would help any, you are welcome to eat in my office."

She gave me a slight smile and said, "Thank you." Nothing more was said between us regarding the situation. My words showed that I was aware of the situation and that I did care.

I had done what I could; now I could only stand back, watch and care. For her own part, Lori continued to eat at the table in the cafeteria – alone.

The year went on and things began to change to the way that they had been. Not completely as they were before, but at least close. Students were beginning to eat with Lori and she was once more a central part of the student activities. One day, when the opportunity arose, I said to her, "I'm glad to see that you are beginning to have friends again." It was hard to know just how to word what I wanted to say, but I did want her to know that I noticed and that I really did care and was glad for her.

"Thanks," she said. Then she gazed at the floor for a moment, unsure how to continue. Then she looked up at me. "One of the things that helped the most was knowing that I had a choice," she said. "A safety net. I knew that I didn't have to sit there alone at that table. I could always go and eat in the office if things got to be too bad -- knowing that made all the difference in the world."

I nodded, feeling so choked up that I was unable to put what I wanted to say into words. The gentle smile that she gave showed that she understood and acknowledged the words that I couldn't speak.

I learned something that day. It is of the utmost importance for educators to provide safety nets. We can't always prevent situations from happening. We can't always eliminate the hard times that our students pass through. Lori taught me that difficult times can be growth experiences that help individuals become the best they can be.

Lori, thank you.

The Refugee

"You can overcome anything if you don't bellyache."
-- Bernard M. Baruch

"Urrr," I groaned as I reluctantly sat up on the edge of my bed. "It's Monday; I hate Mondays!" It was one of THOSE days. We have all had them, the type of day when you focus on all the negative aspects of your life, complain about them and literally brighten a room by leaving. This was my Monday and life was terrible. I was throwing myself a first class pity party. I earned it, I deserved it and by gosh I was going to have it!

"No other teacher in the school could understand what I do each day and how much work I have," I thought to myself, as I went about getting ready for the day. Naturally I managed to trip myself on my own feet which didn't help to make the day any better. "I have four different classes to prepare for, I have the responsibility of providing ESL support for numerous students, I have tests to grade and I can't grade them at home in the comfort of my kitchen because I hate the color of my kitchen; it's blue and I hate blue."

I slammed around getting ready for work, finding fault with my dog, my coffee and everything else; any animate or inanimate object that crossed my path that morning was in danger of being criticized. Like I said, I was having a first-class pity party!

It seemed as if everybody and his brother smiled at me and gave me an especially cheery 'Good morning' that day. "They are so patronizing," I thought to myself while I smiled back and tried to give them each as cheerful a greeting as possible. I felt very self-righteous for doing so. "They all have it so easy, in comparison to what I have to go through every day," I said to myself. "If they had to change places with me, even for an hour, they wouldn't be so blasted cheerful." I placed my books carefully and gently on my desk, praising myself for not slamming them down as I felt like doing. "Gentle on the outside and slamming on the inside," I told myself wryly.

I tried to keep my bad attitude to myself, but as you know, that isn't easy and I had the feeling that my students felt as if they were walking on eggshells. Second period arrived and I thought to myself, "Great! Mohamed is coming and I will have to proofread his English assignment. I have tests to grade; this is so inconvenient."

Mohamed was a student from Somalia to whom I provided ESL support. Mohamed was not your typical 17 year old boy. He was quiet, not in a shy way, but always seemed to be engaged in deep thought. When you looked at Mohamed, his eyes shone with a depth of wisdom that is normally only seen in men who are much older. Mohamed arrived in American schools three years ago and was struggling with academics as well as in acquiring English. Even though he struggled, he had nearly perfect attendance and worked diligently to be successful in school.

"Good morning," said Mohamed giving me a slight smile as he entered the room. He sat down, ready for me to begin proofreading his essay for English class. Mohamed handed me the essay and I began to read it.

In the essay, Mohamed detailed in very elementary English how he and his family arrived in the United States. They were living in Mogadishu, Somalia's capital, when the Somali civil war ignited. He and his family were trying to leave the city for safety when he witnessed his grandmother being shot and killed by anti-government forces. They fled to a refugee camp where Mohamed did not receive any formal schooling and where he had to fight for basic necessities like food and water. Luckily they did not stay in the camps long, were granted refugee status, and settled in Columbus, Ohio. I was so moved by the writing that I literally could not proofread the essay.

I looked up. "Mohamed, you've done well in telling your story," I told him. "You've made me feel something of what it must have been like to face some of the challenges you've had to face." Mohamed, who witnessed atrocities that I could not even fathom, was coming to school each day, working hard and struggling to learn and adjust to a culture that was completely foreign to him. I initially felt pity for Mohamed, but that quickly changed to admiration when I thought to myself, "Here is a young man who fled from a civil war not pitying himself and not allowing the difficult aspects of his life to hold him back, and here I am complaining about the temperature of my coffee." It really put things into a clear perspective.

I managed to proofread Mohamed's essay, "Look here, let me show you how the nouns and the verbs have to match or be in agreement." I walked around and sat down next to Mohamed so that we could both see his paper. I worked with him on noun/verb agreement and sent him back to class. After Mohamed left, I began to grade the tests and I thought to myself, "I really like my job, and blue is a pretty good color for my kitchen."

When I now want to have a first-class pity party, I think of the wisdom demonstrated by Mohamed through his attitude and my party is quickly canceled.

Learning English

"At times, even the best exams cannot measure what teachers know in their hearts."

"Hi, Mr. Poroda," said Nana, entering the room. She slung her book bag down next to her seat and sat down. "Say did you see on TV last night, about Cristina Aguilera? She and..."

"Oh, no, no, no," I told her, laughing as I held up my hand. "Today we are going to concentrate on your Chemistry assignments."

Nana grinned. "But this is much more interesting," she told me, her eyes sparkling with mischief.

"But this is much more necessary," I told her. Nana was a strong, intelligent and social student from Ghana to whom I provided ESL support services. Not that Nana needed much support in acquiring English; she rarely had difficulty understanding either social or academic English; she passed all of her required graduation exams on the first attempt and she always did exceedingly well in each of her classes. But still, until she scored a 'five' on each section – Reading, Writing, Listening and Speaking– of our district's standardized test to determine English language proficiency, Nana was assigned to report to my class one-day a week for ESL support.

Nana grinned. "It was a good try," she told me.

"Yes, it was," I told her. "But it is not going to work this time." Without fail Nana would always come into the room bubbly, full of smiles, whether it was in the regular classroom or in individual tutoring sessions with me. She would always want to share all of her weekend experiences with both her classmates and me.

During the time that I had been assisting Nana with her school assignments; she had consistently tried to get me off-track by quickly summarizing my lesson in nearly perfect English and then trying to get me involved in a discussion of pop-culture, school affairs, or any other topic she thought might get me off task. I hate to admit it, but on rare occasions she was successful and would get me involved in a conversation about Brittany Spears, Cristina Aguilera or other celebrities whom Nana admired before I realized what was happening.

"Cristina Aguilera and Tony Bennett have this thing going," she told me.

"I don't think so," I answered. "Cristina is only in her twenties and Tony Bennett, he's got to be eighty something. You've got to be thinking of somebody else."

"No, I'm thinking of Tony Bennett alright," said Nana, biting her lower lip to keep from giggling.

"It's got to be somebody else," I told her. "Why Tony Bennett, he was popular when my folks..." suddenly I realized what she had done. She'd gotten me again.

"She was in *Tony Bennett: an American Classic* and it just got three Emmys," she told me.

"Yeah, well, he sure deserves it; that guy's been a legend for a long time," I answered, but we'd better get down to business." I didn't want to let her know I was on to what she was up to; that would have taken the fun of the game out of it for both of us.

My weekly visits with Nana were always entertaining. I looked forward to them and I really enjoyed observing her grow as an individual. As spring of her junior year approached, the topic of Nana's conversations changed to be that of career plans and hopes/fears of the future, sprinkled with a bit of fashion and music just to make it interesting. "I've got plans, Mr. Poroda," she'd tell me. "Big plans."

February was the time when we began our district's standardized test in English language proficiency for our non-English speaking students.

Nana faithfully attended each of these test sessions and it was clearly evident that she was doing exceedingly well on each portion of the exam.

"Let me start the tape and then you can respond to the questions," I told Nana. She sat back in her chair with a half smile, waiting to see what the tape had to say.

"Look at this picture. It is a picture of a market," said the voice on the tape. "People buy things at markets. Tell me about the picture. You may want to talk about the types of things you can buy at the market. You may want to talk about the people at the market. . . . " I showed Nana the corresponding picture and paused the

33

cassette recorder in order to listen to and evaluate Nana's response to the speaking component of the exam.

Nana sighed and stated, "Oh my god, Mr. Poroda, this has got to be the dumbest question I have ever heard! Who talks like that? Tomatoes, corn, apples, whatever. Can I tell you about what I heard about Angelina Jolie?"

I laughed. "Go for it," I told her. I didn't start the tape again, and Nana earned a five on the speaking component of the exam.

The Parking Lot

"Fear makes strangers of people who would be friends."
-- Shirley Maclaine

For me, I have always felt more at home in urban environments than in the suburbs or in the country. "Why on earth would you want to live in the city when you can relocate to an area with less crime, 'better' housing and stronger property values?" a friend of mine asked.

"That's simple," I told him. "I like the richness that the diversity of my neighborhood provides me." Then I had to grin. "I don't think I would be able to get Somali chai in a coffee shop or buy authentic tacos from the back of a truck if I lived in a suburban environment."

"Yes, but in the suburbs or the country you'd at least know who your next door neighbors were and you wouldn't have to feel nervous walking down the street in your own neighborhood," he told me.

"I don't feel nervous walking down the street in my neighborhood," I told him. "Yes, you read and hear more about violence happening in the city, but there are more people here also. It's the same everywhere. The city is my home, I really like it here."

One late night I was craving ice cream. I mean really craving it, to the point I couldn't get its icy coldness out of my mind. "Ok, I give in," I said to myself. "I'm going after some ice cream."

I hopped in my car and drove to the local 24 hour grocer. As I was walking from my car to the grocery, I noticed a large, old automobile speeding through the parking lot. It looked like something out of a gangster movie. The windows of the car were tinted so dark that you couldn't see inside the vehicle and the vibration of the music coming from the car seemed to reverberate throughout the parking lot, adding to the car's sinister feeling. Suddenly I was scared senseless. All that my friend had said to me about the dangers of living in the city resurfaced on a wave of fear and apprehension. I fastened my eyes on the store and kept walking. I didn't turn my head right or left; I just concentrated on getting closer and closer to the store. I didn't dare run. I was afraid that might accelerate problems. I just kept walking and walking. The distance between my car and the grocery seemed to have at least tripled in length and I was scared, deep-down-in-the-gut frightened out of my wits.

As the car approached me, the driver slammed on his breaks and I saw the car door open. "My God," I thought to myself. "I'm going to be mugged!"

A giant of a man grabbed me, wrapping his two huge arms around me. I felt the horror of the moment flooding through me, then I heard "Maestro (teacher), ¿Cómo está?" and I found myself embraced in a bear hug. It was Carlos, the father of one of my former students. We chatted for a few moments; he bragged about his daughter's successes at the local university and then left in that big, scary automobile.

Reality and relief sat in. I felt as if I had just walked through a danger zone of some kind and yet I knew that there had been no danger. I felt so absurd, to put it bluntly, I felt absolutely stupid for allowing myself reach that level of paranoia. "I've seen cars like that before and never thought anything about it," I told myself in amazement. "I can't believe I let Doug's comments about the dangers of city living get to me like that. I know better. I really flat out know better. I feel so incredibly dumb." I bought my ice cream and went home.

"I really love city living," I thought to myself.

Everyone's Student
Everyone's Teacher

"It's never too late to be what you might have been."

--George Eliot

"So, tell me about your classes," said Jean, as we played one of our long sessions of Gin Rummy.

"I'm doing pretty well," I answered, trying not to sound too prideful. "I know I'm getting an 'A' in Sociology."

"Oh, I don't mean your marks," she dismissed, moving her hand across the pile of cards in front of her as she spoke. "I know you'll get good marks. I want to know what you're learning." This was Jean all over. She always sought to learn new things, whether it was hearing about the content of my classes, watching CNN constantly, reading, or doing logic puzzles (just to keep her mind sharp). She would use what she learned to make meaning of politics, current events, and personal events that occurred in her life.

Jean left school in February of her senior year of high school in 1940. She had to withdraw from school in order to work and provide support for her impoverished family and she did so willingly, but she has always remained a true seeker of knowledge and is one of the most intelligent people I know.

Jean is my grandmother. Jean was not my teacher in school, but she is my teacher in life.

Gram was a strong teacher, teaching without seeming to teach, by example; by the way she lived her life. Just as she would learn from everyone she came in contact with, she would also teach them by modeling such traits as patience, kindness, respect, tolerance, and a thirst of knowledge.

On her 85th birthday, Gram called me. She sounded excitedly buoyant. "I'm giving myself a special birthday present," she informed me. "I'm going to enroll in the local university and take a few classes."

"Hey, Gram, that's wonderful," I told her, my own enthusiasm matching hers. I couldn't imagine anyone who would get more enjoyment out of taking college classes more than her. "What are you planning to take first?"

"I thought I'd start out with a few classes like Biology and Anatomy and then go from there," she answered. "I thought they'd just naturally lead into what should come next."

"So you're going to be a science major," I said.

"Yes, I guess so," I could hear the enthusiasm in her voice. "But there's something I have to do first. I've got to get my high school diploma."

"So you're going for your GED then?" I asked.

"Yes, the university gave me some information on how to go about that, so I'm going to tutoring. I plan on starting right away."

"That's fantastic, Gram," I told her. "We'll be expecting great things from you."

Gram studied diligently with Sally, a tutor at the local adult training center. After several weeks of preparation, she took her GED and anxiously waited for the results. Two-weeks went by and she found out that she had passed all sections of the exam, except for the mathematics portion. She failed this section of the exam by only three points!

"Oh, Gram, I'm so sorry!" I told her when I found out. "You've worked so hard." I was devastated. Here is a woman who worked so hard her entire life and was unable to pursue her dreams!

"Don't be upset," Gram told me. "It's just one of those things. High school graduation and college just weren't meant to be a part of life, at least not for me." From this comment I saw that Gram's self-confidence was wounded because she was never a woman I viewed as abandoning her goals.

Gram never mentioned pursuing her GED, until about eight months later when I went for a visit and we were playing another round of Gin Rummy. During our game, she said, "I got the nicest graduation card from Sally."

"Graduation card? What do you mean Gram?"

A tear welled in her eye, but there was the sound of triumphant joy in her voice as she answered. "I did it," she smiled, tremulously wiping her tears of happiness. "I graduated from high

41

school." Her smile turned into what I can only describe as an impish grin. "I've been making my morning calls to family and then sneaking off to GED review classes. I didn't want to tell anyone I was continuing to review my arithmetic for the exam in case I didn't pass a second time, but, Jay, I did it. I really did it!'

"Why, Gram, you old sneak you," I teased.

"That's right, and proud of it," she told me, reaching over to play one of her cards.

I was thrilled for her, proud of her and lots of other feelings I just can't put into words. She was and continues to be my heroine. I realized more than ever what it must have cost her as a young woman to leave high school two months short of her high school graduation yet she had done so willingly and with love, bravely assuming her portion of the family expenses.

Gram is now waiting to become a college freshman at 87, every bit as excited as any recent high school graduate. Talk about being a lifelong learner! I am blessed by her example and privileged to be a part of her family.

The Value of Coconut Macaroons

"No act of kindness, no matter how small, is ever wasted."

--Aesop

Noor slouched down in her desk/chair combination and glared at me defiantly. If looks could kill, I would not be here writing this essay. Noor was a young Saudi girl who happened to be a student in my seventh grade Spanish class. I took a deep breath and tried to get myself under control. "Losing my temper won't help matters any," I told myself. Noor had what one of my colleagues had defined as an ATTITUDE when it came to teachers; in fact, if the truth be known, it extended to anyone in the school she viewed as an authority figure. Noor's

43

school life was one of a continually defiant nature, not only with me but with all of her teachers and she had just challenged me in a way that could not be ignored. Had I ignored it, I would have put myself well on the pathway of losing, if not the control of the classroom, at least the respect of all of the students in the class, and that I was not about to do.

While the rest of the class worked on an assignment, I approached Noor and said in a soft but stern tone, "Noor, you will not act that way in this class," being careful to keep my voice at an appropriate level. "I will not lose my temper," I told myself. "I absolutely will not." Besides, if the truth be told, I really didn't feel angry with Noor as much as I did frustration with the situation. I thought of Noor more as a child with a problem rather than a problem child and I wished that I knew some way that I could bridge this gap between us and get her to see me if not as a friend, at least not as an enemy.

"Fine then," snapped Noor. "I'll get out of your precious class." She practically spat the words at me.

"No, you won't," I told her. "You will stay right here in this class and what's more you will not cause any more disruptions."

"I'll get myself assigned to another class for this period," she told me.

"Noor, you and I both know that is not possible," I answered.

Noor dropped her eyes from mine, staring somewhere around my kneecaps. She and I both knew that I was right in my assessment of the situation. She continued to sit slouched down, with her arms crossed and a defiant scowl on her face, but we both knew that I had won this particular battle.

I looked at her for a moment longer to emphasize my point, then turned and headed for the front of the room.

Noor muttered something else. I didn't quite catch what she said although I had a pretty good idea what it was. I started to turn around and ask her what she had said, but then thought better of it. "No sense in getting in a verbal sparring match," I told myself. "At least right now I seem to have come out ahead in this round and it's probably better to leave it that way." I continued with the lesson. Noor discontinued disrupting the class for the rest of the period even though she didn't participate in any of the activities.

"I think this interdisciplinary teaching unit is a great idea," said Mark. He leaned back in his chair in the faculty lounge. "If we can carry a theme through all subject areas, it will give a different atmosphere to the classes, not the usual stuff and just may catch the kids' interest."

"If they're interested, they just might learn something," said Gerry, with a grin.

"God forbid they should actually enjoy studying," Mark continued in mock horror. The rest of the group laughed appreciatively at their joking. We'd all been working on trying to come up with ideas to make the students take a greater interest in learning, not just putting in the time because they had to be there.

"Since the theme is supposed to be *Let's Go Camping*, I think I'll see if I can't get hold of some sort of pop-up tent, bring it into my pre-algebra class and let the students figure out the angles and that sort of thing," said Trudy. "What are you going to do for your Spanish class, Jay?"

"I'm going to teach some sort of a cooking lesson in Spanish," I told her. "I thought I'd bring in the ingredients and let the class make S'mores. You can't get much more 'campy' than that," I said with a grin.

"Maybe you can even get Noor to participate in that class," said Trudy. "At least in the eating part. I don't see how anybody can pass up S'mores."

"How is our problem child doing with the rest of you anyway?" asked Paul. "I'd like to think it isn't just me she hates."

"I had a run in with her today," I admitted. "I managed to keep my hold on the class and put a stop to her creating a disturbance but just barely. I wish I knew some way to get through to her. She's a smart kid; I've seen that spark of interest once in awhile when she thinks nobody's paying any attention."

"Today we're going to make that old camping standby S'mores," I told my class a few days later. "I figured that even if someone doesn't quite understand the recipe as I give it in Spanish, there's no way any of you can manage to poison yourselves with these ingredients." I grinned at my class full of students. "I even managed to bring enough stuff for everybody to make two, so after you've made and eaten your S'more, you can still have some more." The class groaned.

"That joke is pretty bad even for you, señor P," said Derek.

"Hey, don't knock it," said Onari. "At least we get the S'mores."

I passed out the ingredients to each student and then began to demonstrate and give the instructions in Spanish. Soon everyone, with one notable exception, was busy assembling their graham crackers, chocolate and marshmallow treats. Noor didn't participate. She sat in the rear of the class with her arms wrapped tightly across her chest. She glared at me throughout the lesson. It seemed to me there was even more venom in her expression than usual, something that I would not have felt was possible.

Since the rest of the class was busy was the project, I hoped that Noor and I would not be the center of their attention. I stepped over to her desk. "You need to get busy putting that together," I told her. "Those things taste pretty good, too."

"I refuse to have any thing to do with these," she told me, her dark eyes flashing. "I refuse to eat them!"

46

"I am Muslim," she continued. "These contain marshmallows and I am Muslim." There was a certain pride in her tone as she spoke. This was something that went beyond her usual air of defiance; something in her expression seemed to transform her attitude into a righteous one.

Suddenly it hit me. "Marshmallows!" I thought to myself. "Marshmallows contain gelatin which may contain pork. Pork is a dietary restriction in Islam." The anger went out of me like air from a deflated balloon. This lesson was inappropriate for Muslim students. As my grandmother used to say, "I felt like the southern end of a northern bound horse."

"Noor, I'm sorry," I told her. I felt badly about my cultural faux pas and tried to think of a way that I could at least offset it a little bit.

That afternoon I went to a local Middle Eastern grocer to find a gelatin free dessert for Noor. I told the grocer what had happened and he smiled gently. "You are not guilty of being cruel," he told me. "If you are guilty of anything, it is lack of knowledge of Islamic culture and I'm sure had one of us been in your position we could have made the same kind of a mistake when it came to dietary restrictions in your religion. You must not blame yourself."

The grocer went and got a box of coconut macaroons. "These really are a special sweet," he told me. "If anything can get through to your little student, these should do it. At least I don't think she'll refuse them."

I thanked him and went on my way. The next day I brought them to Noor. "Since you were unable to enjoy the S'mores we made in class, I bought you some coconut macaroons instead," I told her. To my surprise, Noor smiled softly.

"This is the first time since I've been in American schools that I have felt special and wanted." She told me, "Always before, I've been different than the others. It's always been as if I'm in my classes but not really a part of them." Noor took the macaroons from my hand and stared at them as if they were made of gold and the look on her face when she took a bite of the sweet was one of pure joy.

"You very much are a part of this class," I told her. "And you are very much wanted and valued in this school."

I walked back to my desk and began the day's lesson, but that day was a turning point for Noor and me. Our relationship changed from an adversarial one to one built on respect. I don't mean that Noor immediately became a star pupil in my class, but she no longer seemed determined to cause a disturbance. She even started to show some interest and slowly began to participate in class discussions. It was evident from her participation that while she had been pretending disinterest in what was going on, she had really learned quite a lot. Noor's attitude towards me slowly progressed until it reached the point where she was outgoing and friendly when I saw her in the hall; it was as if she was slowly becoming a completely different person, at least in my classes.

On the last day of school, I entered my class to find a box of coconut macaroons sitting on my desk. I picked up the note attached and read, "You are special, because you made me feel special. Thank you." I smiled softly, looked at the box of macaroons as if they were made of gold and when I took a bite of the first macaroon, I experienced a feeling of pure joy.

While this may seem to you like a minor experience in a teaching career, it had a profound and lasting impact on me. I learned the real value of Coconut Macaroons. It is not the sweetness of the treat itself that is important, but rather the sweetness of the message that it conveys. It is a message that the small acts of kindness we as teachers demonstrate with our students are not that small and can have a huge and lasting impact on the lives of the students we serve.

May your hearts, classrooms and schools be filled with Coconut Macaroons!

Tough Decisions

"Out of difficulties grow miracles."

-- Jean De La Bruyere

"**O**ne of your children is on the way to see you, Mr. Poroda," said Ernestine, one of the secretaries in my office.

I gave her a slight smile and shook my head. I had recently become an assistant high school principal in a small, urban school district in Western Pennsylvania. It was my first job as an administrator and I was learning the ropes, determined to do the very best I could at this new position.

The secretaries in my office and I would joke that I had several "children." My "sons" and "daughters" were the students who seemed to be sent to the office on a daily basis because of discipline infractions, some of which were minor like sleeping in class to the more serious infractions like fighting.

"You may go in now, Nathan," Ernestine told one of the two boys as she returned to the waiting area where her desk was located.

"Be afraid, be very afraid," intoned Charles, in a low, mysterious sounding voice. Ernestine gave him a stern disapproving look, but inside wanted very much to laugh.

"I got detention," announced Nathan to the room at large, as he came back out and hurried on his way to class.

"Your turn, Charles," said Ernestine, busying herself with the paperwork on her desk.

"I just got a warning put on my file, Miss Ernestine," said Charles when he came back out.

The district where I was working was impoverished and we had to deal with many academic and behavioral issues that only large, urban school districts have the reputation of having, such as high rates of truancy, poor academic performance, drugs and weapons violations. We all, the staff and administration of this school, were highly committed to the students we served and we strove to create a building and an environment that was safe, secure, and nurturing for each of our students.

With this in mind, one of my "children," Beatrice, taught me a lesson that I will never forget.

During her junior year, Beatrice was in my office at least three days a week, mostly for being disruptive in class. Aside from disciplinary issues, Beatrice was doing poorly in each of her classes, not because of lack of potential, but because of a high rate of absenteeism. In order to assist this young lady, Beatrice's mother and I implemented a variety of strategies from one-on-one conferencing, regular parent meetings, behavioral contracts, to suspension, but nothing seemed to work. On the last day of school, I was afraid that Beatrice would drop out and not return at the start of her senior year in high school.

"Beatrice, I'll look forward to seeing you in the fall," I told her, trying to speak casually as we met in the hall.

"Yeah, sure, Mr. Poroda," said Beatrice. She looked up and gave me a hesitant smile, as if she wasn't quite sure if she should say anything or not. "I should think you'd seen enough of me this year to last you for quite awhile."

"I don't mean in my office, unless of course you just feel like stopping by to say hello. You're always welcome. I hope you'll do some really serious thinking this summer. You've got potential, Beatrice. You've got so much going for you. I hope you won't just throw it all away."

"No, I mean, yes, I'll give it some thought, Mr. Poroda," said Beatrice. "I promise, I really will."

On the first day of school, I was pleased to see Beatrice return. I was even more pleased at the end of the first marking period to see that Beatrice had only one minor discipline infraction and that she had made the honor roll. Maybe my interventions were finally working, or maybe Beatrice was finally maturing into a responsible student.

"I want you to know I'm proud of you," I told her, when the opportunity arose for us to chat for a moment. "You've become a student that can achieve both your personal and academic goals and I'm so very, very glad."

"Yeah, well, thanks Mr. Poroda," she told me. I could see that Beatrice felt a little embarrassed at my praise, but I had a feeling that she seemed to be valuing it also. At least I hoped so.

In December, the pride I felt for Beatrice crashed down around me. My day began without incident, but at 9:00 Beatrice entered the office with her hand bleeding. She said she needed to see me.

"Come on, let's get you up to the nurse's office," I told her, hopping up from my office chair. "Call Ms. Dutton and tell her we're on our way to her office, please," I said to Ernestine, as we went by her desk. "Beatrice has hurt her hand and we need to have it treated." Ernestine quickly picked up her phone and started punching in the code for the nurse's office and Maria Dutton was ready and waiting for us when we got there.

"It's a nasty cut, but it isn't deep or anything like that," Maria told us. "You won't need stitches or anything. I can tend to it right here."

"How did this happen, Beatrice?" I asked as Maria was treating her hand.

"It was an accident," said Beatrice. "I accidentally rubbed my hand against the knife I've got in my purse."

"You've got a knife in your purse?" I asked incredulously. Suddenly I felt very sick. This couldn't be happening, not with Beatrice. She'd come so very far.

Beatrice showed me the 6" butcher knife she had in her purse. "I carry it with me for protection when I walk to and from school," she informed me.

"You know that it's against the rules to bring a weapon onto school property," I told her. I stared at her as if I couldn't believe this was happening.

"Yeah, but you know I'd never use it around school," said Beatrice. "I just have to walk through some dangerous places. I really need to have something to protect myself; I really do." Beatrice looked at me as if she couldn't believe that I was objecting to her carrying the knife under the given circumstances.

"We'll talk about this in my office," I told her. "I will come for you as soon as Ms. Dutton is finished with you." I left the room and hurried down to my office, feeling as if I were caught in some sort of a nightmare and hoping I would wake up quickly. "This can't be happening," I thought. "Not Beatrice, she's come so far, she's really trying. This just can't be happening." I went into my office and called Beatrice's mother, explaining tersely what had happened and asking her to join us in my office which she immediately did.

"Mr. Poroda, I can't believe you're making such a big deal of this," said Beatrice, staring at me incredulously. "Come on, please, you know I'm not one of those kind of kids, I'm really not and you know that. I would never, never use that knife on anyone, except to protect myself and then only if I really had to. You can't mean it. Please, give me another chance. There's got to be something…." I had just explained to her and to her mother that I would have to recommend expulsion for one year.

"Please, Mr. Poroda," said Beatrice's mother, the anguish showing in her face. I wished I had someway of making her understand that this was ripping me apart just as it was her.

I shook my head. "Beatrice, you know the rules. You deliberately broke them. I do understand why, but that doesn't excuse what you've done. You could have come to me, we could have talked, and maybe something could have been worked out. I don't know. I certainly would have done all I could so that your walk to and from school wouldn't be a danger for you. But this. . . ." I shook my head again and looked her straight in the eyes. "I'm sorry, Beatrice. I really am."

She heard the finality in my voice and managed to cut off a sob.

53

While I understood Beatrice's perspective, I could not condone or allow a weapon to be brought onto school property. I recognized the strides Beatrice had made, but I had to do what I thought was right for the school and recommend that Beatrice be expelled for one year. Beatrice and her mother begged me not to expel her, but I had to follow my heart, even though I knew that Beatrice would surely drop out of school and not receive her high school diploma. All that potential thrown away!

About a year later, I saw Beatrice and her mother in the mall. "Mr. Poroda!" said Beatrice. She approached me and gave me a huge hug. Her face upon seeing me was one big smile; it was evident that she really was glad to see me.

"Why?" I thought. "I expelled this young lady from school. I had to take a stand that well may have caused her to throw away so much she could have had in life. I know what I did was right, what I had to do for the good of everyone, but still I thought she would hate me."

"You'll be proud of me, Mr. Poroda," Beatrice informed me. "When you expelled me, I realized just how much I was throwing away. I had plans, and they were going right down the drain if I didn't do something about them. I got busy and studied for my GED exam. Passed it with really good marks, too," she added proudly. "And I just finished my first semester in the nursing program at the local hospital."

"That's wonderful," I told her. "And you're right, I am very, very proud of you."

Beatrice hesitated; she looked me in the eye and continued. "I want to thank you for being steadfast in your decision to recommend expulsion," she told me. "I know it was hard for you and you didn't want to do it, but you taught me the true meaning of integrity when you stuck by the rules. You made me wake up and see that I had a choice to either throw everything away or pick up the pieces and put things together in the best way I could. I appreciate you and I want you to know that."

After this meeting I realized that educators are sometimes forced to make tough decisions that can have a huge impact on our students' lives, but if we approach these decisions with care and with the best interest of the student and school in mind, they are rarely the wrong decision.

Sometimes the things that seem to be a person's darkest moments can be the very foundations that lead to the very best.

Stir Fry, Pot Roast, Lasagna and Other Delicacies

"An effort made for the happiness of others lifts us above ourselves."
-- Lydia M. Child

"Of all the stupid jackass things to do," I thought to myself. "I can't believe I did this. Here I am late for school and I've locked my car keys in the house! How stupid can one person be?" I was not my number one fan at the moment. I energetically shook the door knob of my front door, hoping that maybe it would prove not to be quite locked or that it would magically unlock itself and allow me to enter and get

57

my car keys. Since positive thought, jiggling the knob and the sarcasm of a frustrated uttering of "Open Sesame" didn't work, I knew I'd better calm down and take matters into my own hands and find something that realistically might work.

I looked around and noticed that my second story bedroom window was open. "There, I ought to be able to make that ok," I thought to myself. I carefully climbed the overhang of my patio and worked my way over to the half-opened window. "There, that wasn't so hard," I thought to myself, feeling pretty self-satisfied and viewing the problem as already solved. I braced myself and began shoving the window open wider so that I could crawl through. Suddenly my feet began to slide. "Help," I yelled to no one in particular. I tried to catch myself on the window frame but to no avail. I slid from the roof and fell face first to the rock garden below. I was knocked out cold and when I came to, I was one hurting critter. A part of me would have just liked to have laid there but I knew things weren't going to get any better; I needed to do something, so I forced myself to move and managed to make my way to my neighbor's house. I looked like something out of some sort of horror movie at best; my neighbor took one look at me and immediately ran to the telephone and called 911. The folks there immediately had an ambulance dispatched to come to my aid.

"Just take it easy, Mr. Poroda," they told me. "You just lay here and let us tend to everything." One of them fastened a stiff plastic collar around my neck, while the other attached a blood pressure cuff to my arm and started taking my vital signs. In a matter of moments they had me transferred to a rolling stretcher and we were off to the hospital.

As a result of this accident, I missed several weeks of work. I had multiple fractures in my nose, a broken orbital, the boney socket of the eye, and damaged my teeth. I was fortunate that I had not broken my neck. While this was an unfortunate accident, I learned just how generous my middle school students were. Several students sent flowers, cards, and gifts wishing me well.

I returned from the hospital still in quite a bit of pain when one of my students, Mia, and her mother called. "Can we stop by, just for a quick visit?" Mia's mother asked.

"Sure," I told her. I gave her the directions to my home. Actually, I was feeling so sorry for myself, quite understandably if not excusable, that anyone's company would have been preferable to my own at that very moment. When they arrived, I noticed that they were carrying two large boxes. I hurried over and quickly opened the door so that they could come in and set them down.

"Mia, some of Mia's classmates and I spent the weekend making you some homemade TV dinners," Mia's mother told me. "We've got stir fry, pot roast, lasagna and some other stuff so that you can focus on healing and not on cooking. You just take care of getting yourself well and if you need anything please don't hesitate to call us."

"Wow!" I said. "I really don't know what to say. I certainly didn't expect anything like this."

"We didn't know what you'd like best, so we made you a bunch of different stuff," grinned Mia. She looked at my damaged face. "Boy, you really did a job on yourself didn't you?" she said frankly.

"I sure did," I told her. "I'll bet I don't go climbing around on roofs again any time soon."

They stayed for only a few moments and after they left, I dined on a large portion of lasagna. My pain immediately dissipated and I realized that the love and generosity of others really does have the power to heal.

French Class

"Honesty is the first chapter in the book of wisdom."
-- Thomas Jefferson

"M an, I almost feel like I ought to pinch myself," I thought as I walked into the school building. "I've got a job, a real job as a teacher in a real school." I was of course ecstatic. It didn't seem real. Like all students, I worked while going to college in fast food joints and retail jobs. I really looked forward to the day when I'd be a teacher, a real teacher. What made it even more exciting for me was that this wasn't just any school system, but it was the school system of our Nation's capital, Washington, D.C. Public Schools. It was two weeks

61

before the opening of school, and I was on my way to meet with the building principal, Ms. Garret for an orientation session. I passed several people in the hallway on the way to her office and wanted to say to them, "Hey, I'm a teacher, a real teacher." But I managed to refrain and thereby preserve some semblance of my dignity for a little bit longer.

Ms. Garret shared with me an overview of the school's expectations and finally stated, "Mr. Poroda, you will be teaching two sections of seventh grade Spanish, two sections of eighth grade Spanish and one se…..of…..Fr." Her voice went from a very strong confident voice to barely a whisper as she detailed my teaching assignment.

"I am sorry, ma'am. I did not get the last part of my assignment," I said, leaning slightly forward.

"You will be teaching two sections of seventh grade Spanish, two sections of eighth grade Spanish and one sect. . .of . . .Fr. . ." Ms. Garret repeated.

"I am sorry, ma'am, I still did not understand the last part of my teaching assignment"

"One section of French," She replied in a very matter of fact tone.

"Ms. Garrett, I am sorry, but I don't speak French," I responded. "Well, there goes my fabulous new job," I thought to myself. I really was ready to throw myself a first class pity party. I had been so sure that I was starting the beginning of a wonderful new career and now it was all being snatched away from me.

"Don't worry," said Ms. Garret. "You'll do fine."

"I'll do fine?" I asked. "But ma'am, I don't speak French. How can I possibly teach it?" I was totally confused. She couldn't possibly have understood.

"Don't worry," she repeated, "This is middle school French. You'll only be teaching the basic language like colors, numbers and animals. You can do it! Moreover, until we find a teacher who is willing to teach only one period of French, you are the only option we have."

I agreed quickly to the teaching assignment, happy that I wasn't losing my job before I even had an opportunity to begin.

"Welcome to our faculty," Ms. Garrett told me rising with me as I stood to leave. "You'll do just fine."

As soon as I left the building, I headed to the local book store and purchased a language training course in French. I listened to the tapes constantly, rehearsed the dialogues and thought I was ready for my first day of class with the students.

On my first day, all went as expected until French class. I was really enjoying my first day as a real teacher and beginning to feel pretty good about myself. The students entered the room, sat quietly and I began my monologue in French using my best French accent.

"Bonior, class. Jay swee. . . um . Senor …eh I mean er . . Misure Poroda, Jay swee. . . um" The class broke into laughter. I struggled on, all my carefully memorized monologue flying out the window. "Yo est tu, er I mean…I am. . .tu profesore day. . . espa. . um . . . Fransay." By this time the entire class was screaming with laughter. I finished my introduction and stood helplessly, not sure what to do next.

"Mister, that was hilarious," said one girl in the front row. "I know I'm going to enjoy being in your class."

"Err, thanks," I told her, not sure exactly what I should say.

The looks of enjoyment suddenly changed to looks of uncertainty and a few to looks of horrification. One brave young man finally raised his hand. "You did talk like that as a joke didn't you?" he asked. "I mean you do know that you just mispronounced every single one of those words don't you?" (I later found out that these students studied French from first grade!) All of the students stared at me. I think some of them thought it was some sort of a joke and wanted to laugh but weren't sure if they should, just in case my French really was that bad, which, as you know, just happened to be the case.

I looked out over the class. "I could tell them that their teachers have always spoken Parisian French and I speak French Canadian. It sounds plausible, at least sort of," I thought. Then I decided I'd probably just dig myself a deeper hole. I'd always been taught that honesty was the best policy and decided to tell them the truth.

"You are probably right," I said in a humble tone. "I speak Spanish, and I don't speak French at all."

"And you're the French teacher? Come on, you've got to be kidding," said one boy.

"No, it's true," I told them. "I've spent the last two weeks studying French language tapes and when I went to speak to you everything just went out the window." I grinned wryly. "I never wished so hard for a fire drill in my life." Everyone was silent for a moment, and then the entire room burst into laughter, me included. "Don't worry; the school is looking for a French teacher, so this will only be a temporary situation. I know a lot about languages and we can learn about French grammar together in the meantime"

The students seemed fine with my response, and we spent the entire semester working and learning French together. If they occasionally, okay, quite often corrected my pronunciation or managed to try hard not to laugh too hard, they hopefully learned more French in spite of, or maybe even because of my mistakes. The fact that they at times had to teach the teacher may have been a good thing. I never mastered the language, and the school never did find a French teacher. What did occur is that I instantly developed a relationship with this class because I was honest with them regarding my knowledge base.

I am happy that I started off my teaching career in this way, rather than hiding behind some sort of false excuse.

Graduation Day

"What is cynic? A man who knows the price of everything and the value of nothing."

-- Oscar Wilde

I am an administrator for an Adult Education program. Many of the courses in this program are short, practical courses that end with the students receiving certificates of completion that show they have reached a certain level of proficiency in a particular skill area.

While satisfactorily completing a course is something in which the students certainly should take pride, it was not, in my estimation, an occasion for a special ceremony of any kind. I was surprised when, Sara Lee, one of the program's medical instructors approached me and told me she wanted to have a graduation for her class of Phlebotomy students.

"Absolutely not!" I told her. "Not for a three week course where you learn to draw blood." In my mind, such a thing seemed ludicrous and demeaning to the whole idea of graduating. She was persistent and I finally relented and permitted her to plan a graduation ceremony.

As I said, Sara Lee was a persistent devil, and she wasn't satisfied with just getting permission to hold the graduation. She returned to ask me if I would speak at the graduation. Deciding that it would be better to agree than to try to explain my refusal without seeming to downplay the students' accomplishments, I agreed.

There were ten students in the Phlebotomy class and I expected that they would bring a few guests to their so called 'graduation.' I opened the door to the auditorium and was astounded. There were at least eighty people in the auditorium, with banners and balloons; truly celebrating this occasion. It was then that I realized, it wasn't the amount of time that mattered, it was achieving a goal. For many of our students, this was a major occasion in their lives.

It was then that I realized that Sara Lee and the students were not just celebrating the three weeks that they had put into learning how to draw blood; it was the accumulation of other things such as the time they had spent earning their GED, which made them eligible for these classes, or the effort they had put into working to save the money to be able to take these classes, or being able to begin aiming for other educational goals. For many, this was the only graduation in their lives and was as meaningful and as deserved as any other graduation.

Deserve a graduation? Yes, they did. One in which I was honored to have been a part.

"Unless someone like you cares a whole lot, nothing is going to get better. It's not."

-- Dr. Seuss

The Book is Finished. . . ,
the Message is not.

Looking for an inspirational &
motivational speaker on equity, diversity
and intercultural issues in public education?

Have Jay speak at your next meeting!

For information call: 614.397.0946